# That Land I

GW00853557

## Jenni Doherty & Liz Doherty

# Folklore Of Donegal

**Design**
Michael McCarron

**Typesetting**
Joe Mc Allister
Michael Doherty

**Illustration**
Marilyn McLaughlin

# Acknowledgements

Our thanks to Manus Martin and the Training and Employment Agency for their continued support under the Action for Community Employment (ACE) programme. Also to Derry City Council's Recreation and Leisure Department for providing generous Community Services Grant Aid which is greatly appreciated.

Special thanks to the following for their creativity, hard work and dedication to the Press: Fedelma Healy, Sheila Carlin, Carol Hippsley, Fergal MacDermott, Oona Woods, Gerald Hasson, Charles Curran, Martina McLaughlin, Colin Darke and Brendan Brown.

We also wish to express our appreciation to: Tina Farren, Hugh Cavanagh, Mrs Mary Conaghan, Mr and Mrs Diver (Packie Pat), Daniel and Rosemary Doherty, Jim Doherty (Hugie Nellie), John Danny Doherty, Paddy Doherty (Davy), The Dohertys (Rock) from Clonmany, Tom Gallagher, Nellie 'Tarlach' Gibbons, Vincent Harkin, Philip Houton, Marie McCann, Lily and Onnie McGonagle, Vincent and Mary McGonagle, Paddy McGroaty, Frances Mullan, Sandy Peoples, John Wilson, Seamus Canavan and associates, and The North Pole bar in Drumfries.

Also special thanks to the following: Hugo Boyle for the use of folklore material from a radio programme *The Green Microphone* with Father Fitzgerald on North-West Community Radio; Peggy Simpson for allowing the use of extracts from her father's book *Inishowen: Its History, Traditions, and Antiquities* by Maghtochair with original pieces published in *The Derry Journal*.

Designed and published by:
GUILDHALL PRESS
Community Books Publishers
41 Great James Street
Derry
BT48 7DF
Northern Ireland
Tel: (0504) 364413

# Contents

# Introduction

*That Land Beyond* is a collection of stories gathered from throughout County Donegal capturing the beliefs, customs and traditions of rural life down the decades. The stories presented are similar to those told by folk sitting around the fireside at any 'ceilidhing' house in Ireland in centuries past. They depict a time when poverty went hand-in-hand with superstition, a time when it was considered normal to hear the wailing of the banshee or to fear the wrath of the 'wee folk' if you interfered with any of their 'gentle ground'. A spectrum of stories are included covering: the sea and the harsh life of the fishermen; the history behind certain place names; the involvement of historic characters; and how some areas obtained ghostly status or 'holy ground' significance.

The majority of these stories have never been published before and are kept, wherever possible, in the original storytellers' words. It is left to the reader to make up his/her mind as to whether they really took place or not. Many are told by the people involved in the incidents whilst others have been passed down the generations by word of mouth and undoubtedly have been embellished or altered in the narration. But in its way this enhances the drama of the stories rather than detracts from them.

The title of the book, *That Land Beyond,* is the poetic reference people used when talking of the fairies and their mythical world. They believed that by not referring directly to the wee folk by name that they would be protected from their meddlesome and sometimes vindictive activities and that their fear of the fairy world could be concealed.

The origin of fairies is uncertain: some believe they were fallen angels, banished from Heaven after opposing God in battle; others believe that they were the spirits of those who died before Christianity; and in Celtic mythology they were the defeated Tuatha dé Danann who refused to leave Ireland and were thus transformed into fairies.

*That Land Beyond* not only unfolds as a book interwoven with the richness and wonder of custom, folklore and superstition, but it also shows the love and humour shared between people and gives a hint of what life was like decades ago. It sews the threads of human experience together with words passed on like fine silver from one generation to another to reveal some of the secrets of the folk from Donegal and to rekindle the fires of their ancestors.

# Streaks Ahead

In the townland of Shrove lived a family of six. Georgie was the eldest boy and he took pride in being the chosen one to help his father on the farm. He was still at school and was quite competent with the animals so his father allowed him to tend the cows by himself and gave him full responsibility for feeding the pigs and chickens.

It was Hallowe'en day and everyone was excited. There was a lot to be done on the farm and the girls were busy helping their mother with the baking and collecting apples for the night's party games. The McLaughlin children from Carrowhugh were coming to join in the annual fun.

Hallowe'en was known as the most haunted night of the year and the time when the supernatural was at its closest to the world. Due to the many superstitions concerning this night few dared to venture outdoors for fear of all the fairies, witches, ghosts and spirits that might be encountered.

Now Georgie was a bit of a character, dark-haired and fond of mocking these old-fashioned beliefs. He treated Hallowe'en as just a bit of fun; the festivities entertained the children and kept them indoors under the supervision of their parents.

Georgie's house was close to a spot called 'Craic a Mholla', an area of gentle ground where fairies were supposed to live. It was right behind the old schoolhouse and down beside McGonagle's pub, but Georgie had never seen a trace of the fairies. It was just another night for him and the cows needed feeding. He prided himself in being a hard worker, maybe not at school but definitely on the farmyard.

It was dusk. Colour began to drain from the world. The lights of nearby houses sprang one by one into life, piercing the darkness. Georgie had nearly finished his duties for the evening when, all of a sudden, something grabbed hold of him from behind and carried him off to the potato field.

Georgie saw before him a crowd of little people and suddenly regretted he had mocked the stories of the fairy folk. They made him jump every one of the potato pits – his legs weren't that long, so it was quite an ordeal!

Next he felt a huge hand on top of his head, lifting him onto the roof of the old schoolhouse, leaving him there with only a candle beside him.

Apparently this frightening but harmless act was to gain retribution from Georgie's father who had that day accidentally cut down a thorn tree, greatly annoying the fairies. When they spotted Georgie out and about they decided to take their revenge and have a little fun at the same time. After that Georgie took considerable care on Hallowe'en for fear of the fairies stealing him away.

For the rest of his years he possessed five silvery-grey streaks in his otherwise dark hair where the 'hand' of the fairy had lifted him – a true mark of distinction and a highly visible reprimand from the spirit world.

# Patrick's Close Call

Ciaran and Marie Kelly lived in a small cottage in Shrove with their newborn baby Patrick. He was a very cranky child who gave his parents little or no peace.

One fine Spring afternoon Ciaran Kelly was out trimming the fields and thought he'd cut down a small thorn tree that was growing in an awkward position. For once little Patrick had drifted off to sleep and Marie stole the moment to milk the cows. Afterwards, she wandered indoors to see how her son was. Peering into the cradle in the hope of finding the baby asleep she saw a sprig of bindweed in the place of little Patrick.

She alerted her husband and the neighbours in a panic, frantically asking everyone how they could get Patrick back. Wise old Mrs Gibson spoke up, 'Did any of ye do anything on the fairies of late?'

'Ah, not at all. We wouldn't do anything on the fairies. What do you mean woman?' asked one of the men present.

'Well, did ye cut down any trees or bushes belonging to the wee folk?'

Men scratched their heads and the women looked worried.

Then Patrick's father said, 'Aye, come to think of it, I was out cutting bushes earlier. I did move some thorn trees as well but sure there's no harm in that. There's plenty more there.'

6

'Ciaran Kelly,' retorted the old woman, 'go ye now and put that tree back where you found it till you see what awaits ye!'

There and then Ciaran and some neighbours replanted the thorn tree, and when they checked they found little Patrick resting in his cradle.

It is said that, for the rest of his life (and he lived well into his nineties), Patrick Kelly was so convinced of the power of the wee folk after his close call that he never set foot outside the door on Hallowe'en night, for fear of the fairies stealing him away for good!

# Food For Thought

Traditionally, Hallowe'en was the day of the fairies. If you were out on that evening, even if you saw nothing, you would hear the sound of the wee folk singing or chanting melodies. So people were advised to be very careful in case any harm befell them. However, not all fairies were to be feared. If you were generous to them, they would treat you likewise.

In the district of Ballyliffin, one family had experienced many sightings of fairies at the end of one of their fields, close to the house, in what was known locally as gentle ground.

One Hallowe'en night, when the children were gathered for their dinner, they asked their mother about the wee folk.

'If you wait a bit, until the meal is ready, you will see for yourselves.'

When their mother eventually began serving the food, the plates and cups on the dresser suddenly began to rattle and shake until it seemed the whole thing was swaying to and fro. This continued for several minutes and the children became slightly anxious.

'I'll go and give them a wee bit of supper now,' said the mother to the relief of the children, and sure enough, as soon as she had put some spuds out for them, the noisy rattling stopped. 'You should always be good to the wee folk,' warned their mother, 'no matter what, you should be generous with whatever you have. Do you believe me now?'

The children readily agreed and every Hallowe'en after that they would recall in hushed voices the fairies mysteriously moving the crockery and the dresser.

On another Hallowe'en one of the boys from a neighbouring house was out for a walk and happened to be eating an apple. He was passing an area that was renowned as gentle ground when, unexpectedly, a group of what he thought were ordinary people gathered around him. He began to run but they followed until finally, in rage, he threw the apple at them. Once they had the apple they disappeared.

It seems that the boy had never left anything aside for the fairies so they decided to 'persuade' him to be a lot more generous. They took the apple to be a gift and from then on the boy made sure that he kept something for the fairy folk at Hallowe'en.

# Fateful Delay

One evening late in winter, Dan McAllister was rushing home to his house in Glencolumcille. He had stayed longer than he had intended working in the field, and he would miss the fishing boat that evening if he didn't set off right away.

'Don't be rushing, son, sure you have time yet to take a sup of tea,' comforted his mother. 'By the time you are changed and ready, I'll have it made and it won't take you two minutes to drink it.'

The son agreed reluctantly to wait for the tea. He knew that it would be a long night on the boat without something in his stomach. But just as he approached the kitchen the pot of tea that was sitting ready for him toppled from the fireplace for no reason at all.

'Oh Lord!' exclaimed his mother. 'Wait another minute and I'll make you more. The kettle is boiled and it won't take long for you to drink it; sure it would be a shame to send you out in this wile night without anything in your stomach.'

The son again agreed, although he knew that he would have to dash if he were to arrive on the shore on time. True to her word, the mother wasn't a minute making the tea and her son drank it down hurriedly before running out the door.

Seeing that he was indeed going to be late, Dan decided to take a short cut across the fields. However, the resident bull had other ideas and when Dan realised his predicament he turned and ran for his life back the way he had come, just managing to jump the ditch in time. So he would have to go the long way after all. Meeting the bull had made him even later than he had been previously. As he finally reached the pier he saw the boat disappearing around the headland. Dan was disgusted at the line of events that had caused him to miss the boat.

'It was that last cup of tea that kept me late. Sure this hasn't been my day at all!' he fumed.

Dan returned home and went to bed not at all pleased with the day's events. The following morning he realised how fortunate he was to have been delayed when his mother told him – with tears in her eyes – that the boat he had just missed the previous night had been lost in a storm and all on board were drowned. Fate had indeed smiled on Dan McAllister and, for whatever reason, saved him from a watery grave.

# No Smoke Without Fire

There was once a widower called Mick Carlin who lived alone in Letterkenny. His family had all grown up and emigrated as there was little work for anyone in Ireland at the end of the nineteenth century.

He lived in a small thatched cottage which had two bedrooms and one main living area with a large open fire where he made his breakfast, tea and supper. For some time he had been having problems with smoke from the fire blowing back into the living room. The local people who visited him daily were getting very tired of the ever present smoky haze in the room, choking everybody to death. The topic of conversation in the house was always how to fix the chimney, although Mick himself couldn't have cared less. He didn't mind in the least his visitors having to sit in such a foul atmosphere.

The neighbours were finally moved to take action on the matter as conditions in the house were getting gradually worse and they didn't want to lose one of the best ceilidhing houses in the district.

It was decided to write to Mick's son in America who was, according to his father, a bit of a genius. The letter was written explaining the problem and the next day it was posted. It should be noted that Mick had not been consulted about the letter as everyone knew how little he cared about the matter. When the son received the communication he was at a loss as how to respond so he decided to ask his boss whom he considered knew everything about everything. After asking a few questions about the layout of the house and the yard, the boss told the son that the best course of action would be to cut down the tree growing just behind the cottage and the problem would be solved.

When the son's letter arrived back in Letterkenny the people tried to convince Mick that this would be the best remedy for the problem, but he was having none of it.

'Not one of youse had better cut that tree down, for if youse do you'll have me to face!' exploded Mick.

Disappointed, the people put the matter to rest until the next ceilidhing night when the smoke was the worst that it had ever been. They devised a plan. Some of them would keep Mick talking while a few others would sneak out and cut down the tree.

'Sure when he sees the difference it'll make to the fire, it's thanking us he'll be,' said one of the ringleaders of the gang. And so they did as they had planned.

While Mick was inside making his supper of boiled potatoes and talking to a few neighbours that had called that night, the rest went around the back of the cottage and set about the unfortunate tree with axes.

At the time this was all happening Mick was standing by the fireside stirring the pot of potatoes when all of a sudden a terrible wind struck up in the house. Within a moment all the smoke in the room was gone, but still the draught got worse until, to everyone's amazement, the pot that Mick had been stirring disappeared up the chimney and a moment later Mick himself disappeared after it!

Eye witnesses swore that Mick and his supper pot went flying out of the chimney, over the top of the house and landed in a heap near the turf stack! Within minutes the place was deserted as no one wanted to be blamed for the near disaster to poor Mick. It took some time for him to recover, but he made sure that he got his revenge on all the people that were involved that memorable night in old Mick Carlin's house.

11

# Seeing Red

It was a fine harvest day and Tom Doherty was walking in the fields close to his house when he heard a clacking noise in the hedge. Thinking it very strange to hear what he thought was a stonechat singing so late in the season, he crept quietly up to the hedge and peered through it. The noise immediately stopped and Tom's eyes fell on an astonishing sight.

On a small wooden stool sat a tiny old man wearing a crooked hat, a leather apron and silver buckled shoes; by his side a miniature brown jug. The little man filled a cup from the jug, evidently enjoying it, and then began to hammer merrily on the heelpiece of a tiny shoe.

'It's a leprechaun!' said Tom to himself. 'If I'm careful, this could be my lucky day.' He moved a bit closer, watching the little man carefully like a cat watches a mouse. Then he announced, 'God bless you, neighbour.'

'Thank you kindly,' the little man replied, raising his head.

'Isn't it a wonder you are working on a holiday,' remarked Tom.

'That's my business, not yours!' answered the leprechaun.

'Fair enough,' Tom mumbled, 'but tell me, what have you in that jug?'

'Hector beer,' retorted the little man.

'I never heard the likes of it,' answered Tom.

Angrily the leprechaun said, 'Then perhaps you have heard of the Danes? Well, the Danes knew how to make beer from heather and they taught us to do likewise. The secret has been in my family ever since.'

'Will you let me taste your beer?' Tom asked.

'Look here, young man!' announced the leprechaun, 'it would fit you better to be looking after your animals than to be bothering decent, quiet people with your foolish questions. You are idling your time here while your cows are shoulder deep in your father's corn.'

Tom was on the very point of turning around when he caught himself on. At all costs he must keep his eye on the little man, so he grabbed him by the arm, did his best to look as fierce as he could, and shouted, 'Show me where you keep your gold or I won't be answerable for what I do!'

'Run for your life,' cried the wee man, 'there's that cross bull just behind you!'

'No more tricks,' said Tom. 'Show me your gold or I'll set the dog on you!'

'Very well. Come along with me a couple of fields off and I will show you where you'll find a crock of gold!'

So off they went, across fences and ditches and around a crooked bit of bog, until they came to a big field that was full of a giant plant called ragweed. All the time Tom kept a firm grip on the leprechaun.

'Now,' said the little man pointing to the ground at his feet, 'dig here and you will find your crock full to the brim with golden guineas.'

Tom could hardly wait to run home and get his spade but before he went, so he would know the place again, he took off his red garter and tied it around a large clump of the yellow ragweed nearest to the spot indicated by the leprechaun.

'Promise me solemnly that you won't touch the garter,' demanded Tom, knowing that the wee man would be bound by any promise he made.

'I promise,' replied the leprechaun, quite civilly. 'And now I suppose I'm free to go.'

'By all means,' said Tom. 'God speed you, and may luck attend you wherever you go.'

'Good luck to you too, friend and much good may the gold do you when you get it.'

Tom ran home as fast as he could and returned carrying his spade. Back at the field, however another astonishing sight greeted Tom – but this time to his dismay. A red garter similar to his own had been tied around every single growth of ragweed in the field. There was little point in digging up the whole field which contained twenty good Donegal acres, so Tom put his spade on his shoulder and set off for home again.

'The old man tricked me at the finish,' said Tom to himself as he walked along. And as an afterthought he added, 'For a long time to come there will be no shortage of red garters in Inishowen!'

# Marriage On The Rocks

Owen McGonigle, a fisherman from Malin, had had a sorrowful life. He had been married to his childhood sweetheart Aoibhinn, from Culdaff, for just a year when she died giving birth to their first child, Oisin. Owen was heartbroken and swore never to marry another woman, as none could replace his lost love.

Many years passed, and true to his word, Owen never looked at another woman. His relatives tried to persuade him to sell his house on the hill and to start afresh in the village where he could mix with the locals and meet new friends. Owen thanked them but declared that he had no interest in moving to another home. His house on the hill was where he and Aoibhinn had shared a short but beautiful relationship, and Oisin was now Owen's only reminder.

Owen spent as much of his time as he could fishing and was often seen out in his boat in all kinds of weather. One such day, as he was pulling in his net, he thought to himself that it seemed much heavier than usual and presumed that he had made a good catch. To his astonishment, there was a mermaid caught in the mesh. It was obvious that she was injured so Owen decided to take her to his house until she was well. He lifted her tail which had fallen from her once they had reached dry land and left it in one of his outhouses behind the stack of nets.

During the time that they spent together afterward waiting for the mermaid to regain her health, Owen decided that perhaps it was time for him to take another wife. He suggested this to the mermaid who readily agreed. They were married soon after and as the years passed they had two children. Owen had never been so happy – at last he had the family that he had longed for. As time went on, Owen seemed to forget that his new wife had once been a creature of the sea.

One day when Owen was out fishing, his wife decided to tidy the sheds that were full of odds and ends that never seemed to be used. During her search she came across the tail that her husband had placed behind the nets. This unexpected discovery brought back many fond memories of her former life beneath the waves and created such a longing for the ocean depths within her that she set off immediately for the sea leaving her new life behind.

When Owen came home and realised what had happened he was distraught. 'Ah! If only I had hidden the tail better, she would still be here!'

The mermaid was never to return to her home on land, yet she always remembered her family. Every morning, for as long as they all lived, the mermaid placed four fish on four flat stones on the sea shore for Owen and their three sons.

# Stones Of Anger

Stone objects were erected in the time of pagan Ireland and it is considered highly unlucky to interfere with any standing stone, cromlech, dolmen, or megalithic monument of any sort, many of which are still preserved in Donegal.

In the townland of Carrowhugh on the upper road of Shrove lie two such stones. They are set 0.5 metres apart and aligned east west. The west stone is 1.6 metres high by 2 metres wide and 3 metres thick. The east stone is 1.6 metres high by 0.8 metres wide and 0.35 metres thick. They are situated on high ground overlooking the entrance to Lough Foyle.

Although the stones are recorded far back in time, one story traces their origin to the early 1800s. At that time there lived two mighty giants. One lived in Shrove – an exceptionally strong and wicked character. A giant cousin of his lived over in Magilligan. It came about that the two men met with each other and made their dislikes known. They had a fierce row and fell out, the Shrove giant exchanging abusive comments with his cousin in Magilligan.

Time passed and the remarks worsened. The Magilligan giant could take no more. His temper broke and he got hold of two huge slabs of stone and hurled them across the Foyle in the hope of killing the smart-tongued Shrove giant. He missed his shot by quite a distance and so the two of them lived on, continuously bickering and competing against each other.

To this day the Carrowhugh standing stones, thrown in anger over a century ago, lie still and undisturbed in that pleasant townland.

# Sir Cahir's Revenge

Fergal MacDermott was sitting on a rock by Minitiagh Lough in Drumfries, pondering his troubles. 'Tomorrow is rent day and the landlord swears that if we don't pay up he will take everything we have, and then Sheila and myself and our poor children will be turned out on the road to starve, for not a penny of rent have I. Oh! God bless us, that I should live to see this day.'

That was how he bemoaned his fate, pouring his sorrows out to the most beautiful of lakes which seemed only to mock his miseries as it moved beneath the cloudless Donegal sky. On another day it might, with all its beauty, charm away sadness, but today it would not lift the black cloud of despair that hung over Fergal and his family.

Yet Fergal's plight was not as desperate as he had thought. Help was at hand from a quarter he could not have expected.

'What's the matter with you, my good man?' asked a tall, strong, handsome-looking gentleman stepping out from behind a whin bush.

Fergal was not a little surprised at the sudden appearance of the gentleman before him. He wondered whether he belonged to this world or not, but he mustered enough courage to tell him how his crops had failed and how some bad fairies had charmed away his butter. Also how the landlord of Inishowen had been threatening to throw him out of his farm if he didn't pay up every penny of the rent he owed by twelve the following day.

'A sad story indeed,' answered the stranger, 'but surely if you presented your case to the landlord's agent he wouldn't have the heart to turn you out of your home.'

'Heart, Your Honour?' retorted Fergal, not sure how to address this stranger. 'Where would the gentleman of Chichester get a heart? I see Your Honour doesn't know him! Besides, he has his eye on my farm this long time for a friend of his own, so I expect no mercy at all.'

'Take this, my poor fellow,' said the stranger, pouring a purse of gold into Fergal's hat which in his grief he had flung onto the ground.

'Pay the fellow your rent, but I'll take care it will do him no good. I remember the time when I would have hung up such a scoundrel in the twinkling of any eye.'

These words were lost upon Fergal who was blind to everything but the sight of the glittering gold. Before he could unfix his gaze and lift his head to pour out his thanks to the handsome stranger, he was gone. Bemused, Fergal looked around in search of his benefactor and thought he saw him riding swiftly away on a white horse across the mystic lough, wearing a plumed, Spanish hat.

'Sir Cahir O'Doherty, the good, the blessed O'Doherty!' he exclaimed, referring to a famous 17th century Clann Chieftain of Inishowen. Fergal ran home excitedly to share with his wife Sheila the good fortune that had befallen him.

The next day Fergal went to the agent's office to pay the rent, not humbly with his hat in his hand, his eyes fixed on the ground and his knees bending under him, but bold and upright like a man proud of his independence.

'Why don't you take off your hat, fellow? Don't you know that you are speaking to the landlord's representative?' said the agent, a bit put out at not getting the respect that most of the poor farmers reluctantly gave him.

'I never take off my hat but to them that I can respect and love. The eye that sees all knows that I will never have love nor respect for you.'

'You scoundrel!' retorted the man, biting his lips with rage at such unusual and unexpected opposition. 'I'll teach you not to be insolent again. I have the power, remember!'

'At the cost of Inishowen Peninsula, I know you have,' answered Fergal who still remained with his hat firmly on his head as if he was the governor of Donegal himself.

'But come,' said the agent, 'have you got the money for me? This is rent day and if there is one penny of it wanting, be prepared to leave your home before nightfall, for you shall not remain one hour longer in possession.'

'There is your rent,' retorted Fergal with a defiant expression on his face, 'you'd better count it and give me a receipt.'

The agent looked in amazement at the gold – real glittering guineas, not ragged bits of notes only fit to light one's pipe with.

So Fergal went off with his receipt, content that he had paid his debt and proud that he had stood up to the oppressive face of authority. But when the agent went to his desk afterwards he was shocked and enraged to see a heap of wheaten bread cakes instead of the money. He raved and swore but all to no purpose. The gold had become cakes moulded like guineas with the king's head, leaving the agent ultimately liable for Fergal's debt to the landlord. Little did he realise an ancient Irish Chieftain had returned one last time to strike a final blow against the establishment.

# The Fairy Rope

In the late nineteenth century life was very different in Donegal to what it is now. It was hard for many of the families whose only source of income came from either farming, fishing or, in the case of women, sewing. It was the custom for many of the women, having done their chores, to sit at their machines and sew until the 'wee hours of the morning' to complete their batch of shirts. The next morning they would rise early to make the journey to the factory to be paid a pittance for their work.

From Urris the women had to trek barefoot across the Gap of Mamore and on through Desertegney to Buncrana where the nearest factory was situated. They carried the heavy loads of shirts on their backs and on the homeward journey they brought with them that night's material to work on.

It was on one of these early morning walks that Ciara O'Doherty spied a bit of rope by the roadside. As the custom was that anything found on common ground belonged to the person who found it, Ciara decided that she could make good use of the rope, so she picked it up and added it to her already heavy burden.

A week or two later Ciara and her sister Clodagh were making butter. The churn they were using was very old but they could not afford to replace it and up until now they had been able to make minor repairs on anything that had got broken. On this day, however, the churn could take no more; the upper metal ring broke and it started to leak.

'Quick,' said Ciara to Clodagh, 'run and get that bit of rope so we can try to fix this.'

While Clodagh ran to fetch it Ciara was able to hold the churn together without losing too much of the cream. When Clodagh returned they successfully repaired it by replacing the broken metal ring with the rope.

'Now wasn't it a good thing I found that rope,' said Ciara, 'otherwise we'd have no butter for a while.'

The two women continued with their work using the newly repaired churn. After a time they noticed something strange was happening. There

seemed to be far more butter than there should have been for the amount of cream there was. Also, the butter was the finest that they had ever tasted. After much thought and debate the women decided that they must have chanced upon a fairy rope which was indeed good fortune as anything belonging to the fairies was known to have magical powers. Ciara and Clodagh realised immediately that they would have to hide the rope in case anybody tried to steal it, so they made a place for it in the thatch roof, put the rope in, and covered it. They made plans that night as to what they would do with the butter they had made that day – perhaps the local shop would sell some for them.

Amid great excitement, the women went to the shop, sold all of the extra butter and even got orders for another batch on condition that it was of the same quality. The next day they were eager to get started on the churning again so they immediately went to retrieve the rope from its hiding place. To their dismay it was gone. They frantically searched the entire thatch, destroying most of it, before they realised that the rope had disappeared. It seems that the wee folk still had some use for it after all, or perhaps they were just playing games with the two women. Most of the profit made from the sale of the butter went towards mending the roof, and the rest was used to repair the churn.

# Monster Of The Deep

Donegal's coastline borders the Atlantic, the second largest ocean in the world. Many people believe we have only recorded a fraction of the life species that it holds. It may be possible that some of the creatures that are believed to be extinct could still be living at the bottom of this immense ocean.

Four men from Donegal believe they saw one such creature. They were preparing to go out to fish for the day. As they were moving out from Tullagh Bay in a nineteen-foot boat, a rare and wondrous creature surfaced about a distance of 30 feet from them, yet close enough for them to make out its features.

All the men on board were seasoned fishermen and none of them had seen anything like this before. Although they could only see its head, it was pulling a wash of about ten feet behind it, which would also indicate that it had flippers of some sort. Its head resembled that of a horse and it had a long thick neck. The men became nervous as the animal seemed to be approaching them so they turned their boat back to shore. The creature then submerged and went under the boat to reappear on the other side, always keeping the open sea behind it. They watched the creature for about 15 minutes and were all glad to reach the shore safely.

Some of the men were reluctant to talk about this unusual experience but eventually the story came out. Instead of ridicule and mockery, their account was actually confirmed by a few of the older people in the district who said that they could remember their parents talking about a creature similar to the one the men had described. They said that it had killed two people who were gathering winkles on some rocks near the water although admitted that no photographic evidence of the creature existed.

However, as in the case of the Loch Ness Monster, even photographs are not accepted as solid proof in such extraordinary circumstances.

# Light A Penny Candle

There was a time when people would never turn away or refuse a stranger at their door. They would always welcome them into their homes with the offer of a meal and a bed for the night – even if they were not well off themselves. For all they knew their visitor could be a fairy testing their goodwill, and if they were unkind or unwelcoming ill fate could befall their family and livelihood.

There was no mistaking Danny Mac when he came to the village of Carrickmaquigley in the land of Drung outside Redcastle some 100 years ago. He was a travelling man, what people then called a 'pedlar'. He traded his goods in Carndonagh and Moville on market days and was a well-known and well-liked character.

There was a household in Carrickmaquigley that always bid him good tidings when he was in the area. They had become accustomed to his regular visits and treated him more as a guest than a travelling man. He no longer graced the corner of the kitchen on a bed of straw for his nightly sleep but lay in relative comfort in the half-loft above the kitchen.

One day, Danny Mac had great success at the trade and made himself a small fortune. He was content with his takings but little did he know that two local men had been spying on him for the best part of the day and were aware of the amount of money he had made. They, too, were pedlars and had also been given lodgings for the night in the same house as Danny Mac, though they stayed below in the kitchen.

In the middle of the night when all were asleep, the two lads crept up the ladder in pursuit of the successful trader's wealth. There was only one other person lying there – a young girl. They checked if she was asleep by lighting a candle in front of her but she never twitched an eye nor moved a limb.

Over they crept to Danny Mac, stole his money and strangled him in cold blood. Between the two of them they managed to carry his body down the ladder and out of the house. No moon or stars were visible that night so they had brought a candle shielded by a jam-jar to guide their path. They went a short distance up the hill in the direction of Gleneely, stumbled over a field to a place where unbaptised children were buried and dropped poor Danny Mac into an open grave which they then filled in. Once they had disposed of the body they disappeared from the village.

To this day there have been numerous witnesses from houses nearby and fishermen on the Foyle who have seen a light moving about this particular place in the dead of night at different times of the year. It is said to be the 'Pedlar's Light' seeking freedom from the graveyard where Danny Mac was left that night.

# Love You To Death

There was once a fisherman, Bill Quigley, who lived on Aranmore Island. He was a poor man who depended on the sea for his livelihood, especially if his crops failed. Normally either the land or the sea would be enough to keep him from poverty, but one particular year both failed him. The weather had been disastrous and no matter how long he persevered at sea he failed to catch even a handful of fish but still he had to try as his only alternative was starvation.

An event was about to occur, however, that was to change his fortunes, and his life, entirely. While he was out enduring his hardship at sea one day, a sea maiden rose from the waves at the side of his boat. Bill was so engrossed in his own desperate situation that even the appearance of a water spirit did not startle him. She asked him politely if he was catching many fish, and he replied dejectedly that luck and fortune had truly forgotten him and things could only get worse.

'What reward would you give me for providing plenty of fish for you?' asked the sea maiden.

'Ach!' said Bill, 'I have not much to spare.'

'Would you give me the first son you have?' queried the maiden.

'I would if I were ever to have a son,' he answered.

'Go home and remember when your son is twenty-years old to send him to me and you will have plenty of fish after this.'

Time passed; everything happened as the sea maiden had predicted and Bill caught plenty of fish and even his crops were good. He married a local girl and reared several children.

Bill never related his encounter with the sea maiden to anyone. As the twentieth year approached the old man became increasingly sorrowful and heavy of heart, and found no peace or contentment day or night. The eldest son Diarmaid, noticing his father's distress, asked him one day, 'Is there anything troubling you?'

The old man replied, 'Yes there is but that is nothing to do with you or anyone else.'

The son insisted and the father eventually told him the story about the sea maiden and the deal he had made with her.

'Let that not trouble you,' comforted the son, 'I will not oppose you.'

The father, whose grief had overcome him, cried out, 'You shall not go! You shall not go, my son, should it mean I never fish again!'

Diarmaid replied, 'I think it is time for me to grasp my own fate and go to seek my fortune wherever it lies.' The next morning he saddled his father's black horse and he took the world for his pillow.

He had been travelling on the road some time when he chanced upon

the carcass of a sheep. A great black dog, a grey falcon and a brown otter were standing around the carcass arguing over who should get what share. They stopped Diarmaid and asked him to make the decision. He came down from his horse and divided the carcass with his sword, giving three shares to the dog, two to the otter and one to the falcon. The animals were so pleased to have the argument settled that they decided to reward him for his good deed. If ever he were in need, the otter promised to help with swimming skills, the falcon with swiftness of wing, and the dog with fleetness of foot.

On hearing this, Diarmaid thanked them wholeheartedly and continued onwards. After a time had passed, he met and married a king's daughter. On the day his father had promised him to the sea maiden, Diarmaid and his wife happened to be walking along the seashore. Before they had gone very far the sea maiden appeared from the waters and seized Diarmaid, without leave or asking. The princess was heartbroken about her one and only love and was inconsolable in her grief. She took her harp to the seashore and played continuously in the hope of comforting her husband and in some way being close to him.

After a time, the sea maiden was so enchanted with the music that she rose from the waves in order to hear more clearly.

The princess promptly stopped playing and refused to continue. 'No, not until I see my husband again,' she demanded.

So the sea maiden reluctantly revealed Diarmaid's head above the water. The princess played on for a short time and then stopped again. 'I will not continue until you take him out completely,' she insisted.

The sea maiden responded by raising Diarmaid above the water but only to waist level. The princess continued to bargain with her until she eventually brought Diarmaid fully out of the sea and onto the shore. The maiden, in her greed, decided that the princess would be a much better catch than her husband, so she left him on the shore and took her in his place.

When the news spread about the sea maiden's treachery there was great mourning in the area. Diarmaid spent so many lonely days and nights wandering up and down the shore searching for his wife that he began to lose all hope of ever seeing his young love again. Then one day he chanced upon a strange little man who was familiar with his predicament. He began to tell Diarmaid about the only possible way of regaining the princess and ultimately his happiness.

'In the island that is nearest to the shore there is a white-footed bird with the slenderest of legs and the swiftest step; and though she be caught, there may spring a houdi [the soul of a spirit] out of her; and though the houdi be caught, there may spring a trout out of her; and though the trout be caught there may be an egg in the mouth of the trout. The soul of the sea maiden will be in the egg and if the egg breaks she is dead.'

Diarmaid then decided to call on the great black dog, the falcon and the otter for help. They dutifully came to the rescue. Diarmaid mounted his horse and jumped the narrow strait onto the island. The black dog took off after the white-footed bird and soon had it trapped. Suddenly, just as the strange little man had predicted, the houdi sprang out from her and into the air. The grey falcon with sharp eye and swift wing tracked the houdi and quickly brought it to earth, whereupon out jumped the trout into the sea. The otter pursued and caught the trout which it then dragged ashore. At once an egg appeared from the trout's mouth. The sea maiden, realising that her secret was out, emerged by Diarmaid's side and begged him for forgiveness and to spare her life.

'Break not the egg and you will get all you ask,' she pleaded.

But Diarmaid took no pity on the selfish and greedy creature who had caused him such pain and sorrow.

He demanded the return of his beloved princess. Before he could utter another word she appeared before him. Diarmaid gazed longingly at her, then lifted his foot and slowly crushed the egg that held the soul of the sea maiden. Diarmaid and his princess left the island and travelled home, never again to be disturbed by scheming female spirits from the ocean depths.

# Dark Dealings

In Milford, around the late 1800s, a young man named Neil McCafferty was on his way to visit a few friends who lived close by. It was getting dark as he came to a crossroads where he noticed they had already gathered. A table had been placed by the roadside and they seemed to be waiting for him. As he drew near one of them said, 'Good to see you, Neil, would you like a game of cards with us?'

'Surely to God I would,' replied Neil, taking his place at the table and they began to play with only the moon for light. After two or three games Neil seemed to be on a winning streak. As the fourth hand was being dealt, one of the cards fell to the ground. When Neil reached down to pick it up he saw to his horror that the 'man' he was sitting opposite had cloven feet. Neil was terribly frightened – the thought that he might be playing with the devil and his cohorts instead of his friends was too much for him and he collapsed unconscious at the table.

When he came round he was alone but thankfully unscathed. He made up his mind that from that day on he would never play another hand of cards for it was one thing to lose your wages to your friends but quite another to risk losing your soul to the devil.

# Blind Man's Bluff

When the railway was built in Donegal many people were delighted at the development. It gave them the opportunity to travel longer distances without having to spend hours walking or cycling – their normal modes of transport.

However, there was cause for dispute when it was discovered that the engineers intended to run the line through an area where a fairy tree was growing and which was said to be used as a crossroads by the wee folk themselves. Quite a few of the locals were working casually on the job clearing away the ground, and it was their duty to destroy the tree. But to the foreman's amazement all his men refused to approach it. They tried to explain to the foreman that to interfere with it would induce bad luck, but he was not from Donegal and had little time for these local superstitions. He threatened the men with the sack if they dared to disobey his orders, yet they appeared quite prepared to lose their jobs rather than venture near the tree. The foreman saw little sense in dismissing all the men as it would take more time to replace them than he could afford. He decided that the best course of action would be to perform the job himself. After all, it was only superstition, wasn't it?

As the foreman was preparing the dynamite to clear the ground it exploded for no reason, leaving him blind for the rest of his life. Apparently, a short time before the incident, one of the local men had seen a group of fairies dancing and singing around the tree in what had obviously been some kind of warning. Unfortunately this had been ignored with dire consequences.

# The Holy Spirit

There was once a man called Bob Donnelly who lived in the west of Donegal. He was a very religious person and every day he would go to the church to pray. Late one particular evening he was deep in meditation in the chapel when he heard a noise coming from the direction of the front door. Thinking it was just someone entering, he ignored it. However, when no footsteps echoed down the aisle he looked round, only to see the main doors being closed by the caretaker. He rose quickly and hurried to the door calling on the man to stop, but he was too late: the doors had been closed and he was locked in. There was nothing for him to do but take a seat and wait until morning. He used the time to pray.

As midnight arrived the vestry door suddenly opened and, to Bob's amazement, out stepped a priest. He came onto the altar and asked, 'Is there anybody here to clerk Mass for me?'

When no one answered, he asked again and then a third time without reply before returning to the vestry.

Bob spent a sleepless night huddled on one of the church benches, somewhat perturbed by what he had just witnessed. When the caretaker eventually threw open the doors the next morning he got an awful fright when Bob rushed out.

'What happened to you?' he asked.

'I was locked in! Didn't you hear me shouting at you last night?' replied Bob.

Bob recounted in detail what had happened, and added that he was going to see the local priest immediately. After listening carefully to his story, the priest asked Bob to return with him that night to the church to see if they could find out more about this strange apparition. Bob was reluctant to go but agreed in the end.

They were kneeling together in the church at midnight when the mysterious priest appeared again asking if there was anyone present who would clerk Mass for him. Once more he asked three times, and on the third occasion the priest stood up and said, 'I will.' He told Bob to stay where he was and went to the altar where Mass was said.

When it was over the ghostly priest exclaimed, 'I have been in limbo here for eighteen years because I died before I could say my daily Mass. Thank you for your help – now at last I will get into heaven!'

He then returned to the vestry and was never again seen. The priest and Bob discovered that eighteen years previously the local priest had died of a heart attack one Christmas Eve before celebrating Midnight Mass and it seems his spirit remained restless because he hadn't performed his Christian duty for the congregation. At least now he would be able to enter heaven with all his obligations fulfilled.

# Double-Take

In the district of Rathmullan about 110 years ago, Milly McLaughlin, her brother Rúari and sister Ann were sent by their mother to the shop to fetch some vegetables. The route to the shop took them along the Shore Road overlooking the sea. They were glad to escape the gloom of the house as their other brother was very ill and their mother spent most of her time fussing over him. After they had gone a distance from the house their mood lightened. They were quite young and could be forgiven for being so heartless as they did not realise how seriously ill their brother was.

They reached the shop and collected the goods. On the homeward journey they were laughing and joking among themselves. All of a sudden they fell silent at the sight of a boy, much their own age, rushing past them. On any other occasion this would hardly have been remarked upon, but a few things about the incident stood out.

The fact that the boy was barefooted was uncommon for the type of day it was, but by no means unusual for the period. The fact that there was no warning of his approach could have been explained by the noise of their merriment. However, one fact stood out from the rest. All three agreed that the boy looked remarkably like their brother who was supposed to have been sick in his bed at the time.

'Heavens Almighty, would you look at where our Jimmy is, and him that was in his bed when we left,' remarked Ann.

'What is he doing going down by the pier?' inquired Rúari.

'We had better stop him anyway,' Milly replied, and she started to call out to her brother to wait.

'Come back, Jimmy. Take your time,' she called but he seemed not to notice. He went on in the direction of the pier and then turned down out of sight onto the beach. The children ran to the shore but there was no sign of their brother. They continued on their way, and after reaching home Milly asked her mother, 'Has anyone been here since?'

'No,' replied her mother.

'Where is Jimmy, is he still in bed?' Milly then inquired.

'Aye, he is still in bed, he never rose at all,' her mother answered.

Although the children were puzzled by the incident, they thought little of it until the following week when their brother died. It was only then they realised that the sighting of the barefooted boy had been a sign warning them of their brother's imminent death.

# Columcille Myth

Clonmany is surrounded by perhaps the most rugged, wild and romantic scenery in the whole of Ireland. Although today it is much more developed and cultivated than it was a century ago, in many places it remains the same, touched only by the endless crashing of the waves on the rocks or the beating of the wind against the hills.

In the district of Straid, some distance from the coast, stand the ruins of an old church said to have been founded by Saint Columcille during the time he spent in the area when he first began his studies for the priesthood. Tradition has it that as he was travelling the countryside he came through Tullagh Bay and Binion late one evening and stopped for a drink from a well near the ocean's edge. The fresh-water well is still in existence today although at high tide it is completely covered by the sea.

The people of the parish decided to erect a church in the saint's honour close to the spot so the local men spent a full day marking out the foundations with sticks and string before retiring for the night.

However, when they returned to the site the next day to commence digging they were amazed to find no sign of their work. Greatly puzzled, the men discussed what should be done. They had more or less decided to begin work again on the original site by the sea when one of the men from Straid said that he had seen new foundations marked out there on his way to work. The man showed his friends where he had seen the markings and they agreed they were laid out as well as those they had done themselves.

While they were standing around discussing what had happened, one of the local women arrived to say that the previous night a great flock of birds had been seen above the well by the sea and that they had moved inland from there to Straid. The people decided that it was an act of God and that for some unknown reason the church was destined to be built at Straid.

They duly built the church on the new site which proved to be a wise decision as the original location is now covered by the sea.

# A Date With Death

On one occasion, in the district of Glengad, Sam Farren was on his way to meet the boat when he spied a fishing net by the roadside. Thinking it strange that someone should discard such a good net, he picked it up and put it on his back, deciding to use it that day. He hadn't got very far when he noticed that his burden was getting very heavy. However, being a strong man, he continued on his journey.

It seemed that the closer Sam came to his destination, the heavier his net became until at last he had to stop. When he tried to lay it down he found it impossible. Suddenly he realised that he had taken a net belonging to the fairies and that he would not be able to get rid of it unless he left it back where he had found it. He knew that he would miss the day's fishing by returning the net but he thought it would be better to keep on the right side of the fairies.

On the return journey, as Sam approached the place where he had found the net, he felt the load getting lighter. When he eventually reached the exact spot he threw down the net and went home.

The next day Sam thanked God and anyone else that had anything to do with his finding the net when he heard the news that the boat he was to go out on had sunk at sea with the loss of all hands on board. If he had not found the fairy net he would surely have been among them.

# Lough Foyle Myths

According to tradition, Lough Foyle takes its name from Loch Feabhail-Mhic-Lodain meaning the Lake of Feval, son of Lodon – a Tuatha dé Danann who drowned in the river. His body was washed ashore by the waves which, in turn, rolled a large stone over it as a monument.

Lough Foyle is also recognised as meaning 'borrowed lake', a name which comes from the story of two mythical sisters who lived beyond the Shannon. The elder of the two had asked the other for the loan of her silver lake, promising to return it on the following Monday. The younger girl rolled up the lake in a sheet and sent it to her sister. However, the elder sister was deceitful and when the time came to return the lake she replied:

'Truly I said Monday (Dé Luain) but I meant the day of judgement (Dia Luain) so I shall keep the lake.'

And so to this day the 'borrowed lake' survives in the Northwest as Lough Foyle, whereas a dried-up lake along the Shannon lies barren and bare.

Lough Foyle has another myth attached to it – that of a Storm God who lies buried in the Tonns sandbanks which stretch along Magilligan Strand for three miles. He was originally believed to have been a Tuatha dé Danann chief who fell in battle fighting for the Milesians. After his death he was defined as a sea sprite – Mac Lir or Mac Lear signifying 'Son of the Ocean'. Inis Manannan (the Isle of Man) is believed to have got its name from the Lough Foyle Mac Lear. Manannan Mac Lear is regarded as the Irish Neptune and it is said that his spirit is freed during fierce storms off the coast of Inishowen Head.

In Celtic mythology it was believed that when Cuchulain hit his shield with his sword the three waves of Ireland would rise up and answer him. They were located at Dundrum Bay (The Wave of Rury), at Cape Clear (The Wave of Cliona) and at the Tonns bank (The Wave of the North).

Every so often the spirit of Manannan Mac Lear comes forth and even yet, just before a storm actually breaks, the Tonns rise up and their roar can be heard for miles around. Local people used to remark, 'Manannan is angry today,' whenever the sea was rough and the weather bad. They would look out the window to see the waves crashing against the Tonns and whisper a silent prayer for anyone caught out on the raging ocean.

In the 19th century there were numerous shipping disasters off the Donegal coast. Many of the local fishermen and sailors were frightened to go to sea because of the Tonns bank and because of the myth of Manannan Mac Lear's spirit.

About the year 1771 around 100 seamen – all from the Moville, Greencastle and Shrove area – were lost in a tragic accident leaving 66 widows. It was remembered as 'Black Saturday' and all the men perished in the Tonns, except one. His name was McGuinness and he managed to drift ashore at Magilligan Strand on an oar. There he saw the strange sight of all his companions walking normally along the beach with their arms folded. The vision may have been due to the effects of his ordeal, although many believe that the men did not drown but instead were carried off by the inhabitants of an enchanted castle.

The next disaster occurred in January 1831 and is remembered as 'The Big Drowning', with 21 boats destroyed. All the vessels were from Greencastle and Shrove, and were returning from the fishing grounds when a hurricane blew up. One man managed to swim ashore but before he could be rescued he was killed on the rocks. From this single disaster 70 children lost their fathers.

In March of the same year there was another apparent sea disaster with about 30 fishermen believed dead, mostly from Moville, Greencastle, Shrove and Drung. A public mass was said for them in Ballybrack Church in Greencastle and for all the bereaved families.

A week or so later many of the presumed 'dead' men came marching up the main street of Moville, to the shock and surprise of all. What had actually happened the previous week had been the fault of two Spanish sailing ships. They had accidentally caused the fishing boats to capsize out by Malin Head but had managed to rescue a number of the men. Because of a strong gale, the sailing ships couldn't turn back to release the survivors on the Donegal shore. Instead, they sailed on until they reached a port in County Mayo where they landed the men for their journey home.

There were no telephone communications at that time so families and friends of the rescued were unaware that their loved ones had survived. Some of them had given up hope and even went as far as getting married again! Of the rescued men, several never returned home to Inishowen at all but stayed in Mayo to begin a new life, forgetting their home town and grieving families for ever.

# All At Sea

It had been a fine day for work and the men of Urris in the townland of Clonmany were tired but happy with their efforts. They had been up with the sun and spent most of the day in the fields thrashing corn. Most of the crop had been saved and the men were relieved, for the weather could break at any time and that would have meant the end of it.

It was now dark and Pat was making his way home from Lenan to Roxtown where his wife would have his supper ready. It was a fine, clear night with a bright moon, and Pat was looking forward to the walk home. His only fear, if any, was of being waylaid by thieves as times were hard for everyone.

Pat was a huge man, over six-foot tall, and the many years he had spent working in the fields since he was a child had made him very strong. It would be a foolish person that would try to rob Pat for the community knew that although he was a quiet man by nature, when he was riled he would put the fear of God in anybody. This night, however, the danger lay elsewhere, as he was soon to find out.

The journey home should have taken him half-an-hour and Pat was beginning to suspect that something was amiss. By now he should have been within a short distance from his house, but instead found he could see none of the familiar landmarks. He was beginning to get worried but decided that he would continue on for another while. Perhaps he had taken a wrong turning along the way, although he couldn't see how as he had walked that same road many times and had never lost his way before.

Pat could hear the roar of the waves in his ears and thought perhaps that he was close to home. He continued until he came to a wild thrashing sea, one that he had never seen or heard before and it was then that he realised that it was the wee folk trying to spirit him away.

Pat had come such a distance that if he was to be saved at all he needed to act quickly. He removed his hat and his coat, turned them inside out and put them on again. Immediately he recognised that he was at Pollan Bay instead of Roxtown and was almost waist-deep in water. Had he waited longer he would surely have drowned. However, now that he had protected himself from the fairies, he was able to make his way home successfully and all was well.

# Earth, Wind And Fire

There are many stories told by people living throughout Donegal about the wee folk and how, if they were crossed in any way, punishment of some kind would follow. In most cases warnings were given by neighbours or an older member of the house.

A farmer from the outskirts of Manorcunningham was troubled about the amount of ground taken up by large flagstones arranged in a circular design in the centre of his field. When he entered the field with his tools and approached the ground, he was showered with stones from every direction. It was a flat field and there was certainly no place for any mischief-makers to hide. The farmer had to flee to escape injury. He decided to leave the stones undisturbed and was troubled no further.

Despite modern society's belief that these incidents only occurred in the distant past, there have been quite a few reported recently.

In the district of Annagh in Clonmany, around 1985, workmen were quarrying in an area that was considered fairy ground. Their mission was to cut down a holly bush that was in the way of their work duties. Neighbours in the area begged the men to leave well alone as there would be serious repercussions if they carried on. The men scorned the locals, retorting that in this day and age there was nothing to fear. But they were soon to be proved wrong.

At the time they were using a JCB digger to clear the land. As soon as it touched the fairy tree the hydraulic system failed. Once they had it repaired they again set out to remove the tree. This time, before the JCB could approach it, one of the caterpillar tracks snapped, something that would take nearly an explosion to do. The men began to have their doubts and remembered the words of warning from the locals. Fear of the unknown enveloped them in a wave of better judgement, but it was too late – the wee folk had already dished out a handful of sweet revenge, as the driver of the JCB was later to find out. He arrived home that evening to discover that his house had burned down and he had lost everything he owned.

It took an occurrence as grave as this to convince those who did not believe in fairies that there was something supernatural lurking in our world that can and will dispense its own powers when it is disturbed or threatened.

# Death Lights

A group of men from the Gweedore district discovered that they could profit from selling the 'Cloch Bán' (white stone) that was being quarried in their local area. They were told repeatedly about the dangers of handling or upsetting the stone which was said to be on 'holy ground' but they ignored the warnings. Money was too easy to be made out of the venture and this opportunity was too good to give up. Only a few of the men eventually dared to go near the quarry, but there were enough of them to remove some of the rock which they quickly sold.

Unfortunately they all suffered the consequences as they suddenly fell ill with a mysterious illness that no one could cure. Within a week their health rapidly deteriorated and they died in inexplicable circumstances.

Many people talked later in hushed whispers of the strange lights they had witnessed surrounding the houses where the men had lived. These lights were too high off the ground to be lanterns, and because of the shape and shadows that followed the lights it was certainly not the result of faulty electricity. Those who observed the peculiar beams recognised them for what they were – death lights which sometimes appeared by a house when someone was going to die.

There are many stories told of lights appearing and floating around houses. They are thought to be the work of the wee folk who would surround the house with balls of light to let the people know a death was about to occur and to warn the community to leave well alone or answer for their interference.

# Mass Rocks

During the Penal days the faith of the population of Ireland was put to the ultimate test – and survived. At that time, to openly practise the Catholic faith was to court death. This, however, did not discourage the population. They selected secret places hidden in the hills, woods or valleys to gather and celebrate Mass, often despite great peril. Evidence of these terrible days lie all over Inishowen in the form of Mass Rocks and holy wells. Several lookouts would be positioned around the place of worship, and at the first sign of danger the alarm would be raised. These isolated sites sometimes witnessed cruel and vile acts perpetrated by soldiers who either discovered the gatherings by luck or by guidance from others.

In Kinnagoe, as elsewhere, the people practised their faith at Mass and the authorities let it be known that anyone prepared to divulge the whereabouts and the time of these congregations would receive a handsome reward. As in all times of peril and hardship there are those who are ready to betray their beliefs and neighbours for their own personal gain and Anne McGuire was one of them.

McGuire decided that the offer was too good to turn down, so she met the soldiers in secret and they proposed a plan to trap the lawbreakers. She described exactly where the Mass Rocks were in a particular part of the hills and the next time Mass was due to be said she arranged to hang a white linen wash on her line as a sign to the soldiers.

When the occasion eventually arose, McGuire put out the linen as planned and continued about her normal everyday tasks. On seeing the prearranged signal, the soldiers set off immediately towards the area where the Mass was supposed to be taking place. However, as they passed close to McGuire's they noticed that it wasn't material on a line at all but a slab of white rock beside the house. Thinking that they had simply made a mistake they returned to barracks.

When Anne McGuire came home from Mass she discovered that her linen had been turned to stone. At once she was repentant of the evil deed she had committed and went directly to the local priest to confess her sin. To this day the 'stone washing' can be spotted on the face of a rock outside Carndonagh.

Many people believed that Mass Rocks, and the ground surrounding them, were special places. To interfere with them would be to risk disaster.

In the outskirts of Carndonagh one of the local men, Tom McAdams, had been called out late one night to help with a cow that was having trouble calving. On his way back home he had to pass by the site of an old Mass Rock. At the time the men were working on building a new road which meant that they were disturbing the ground around the rock itself. All of a sudden, Tom heard the sound of people talking and as he came closer to the Mass Rock he saw a large crowd had gathered. Thinking that something was amiss, he went closer to investigate and realised that he recognised some of the faces. Strangely, this did not reassure him as he still felt something was not quite right. Then it suddenly hit him – the people he recognised had been dead for years!

Not wanting to interfere with the ground and whatever was happening, Tom quietly slipped away and returned home, where he told his wife what he had seen. She said that it was a sign from above and that the work should be stopped. When the builders heard the story the next day they all agreed to down tools. The ganger wasn't too pleased and had no option but to change the course of the proposed road away from the Mass Rock area.

# Horse Sense

One day Alan Hasson was coming home from his work in the fields on a cart pulled by two horses that he had just used for ploughing. He was hungry after his hard day's labour and was looking forward to his dinner. But when he reached the spot where he normally forded the stream, for some reason, the horses would not cross. Alan tugged at the reins but still they would not budge. Wondering what to do, he looked around and spotted a young boy a short distance away. Alan decided to lead the horses across the stream one-by-one and made to approach the boy for his help. It was only then he noticed that what he had believed to be a boy was in fact a small man. He also noticed that, although he was walking towards the man, he did not draw any nearer to him. He started to run but still he got no closer. The small man then walked behind a rock and when Alan finally reached it he had completely vanished.

Puzzled, Alan returned to his horses. This time they moved with no hesitation across the stream. It was then he remembered his father say that although humans can sometimes see fairies, animals can always sense their presence. So if you are ever riding a horse and it stops for no apparent reason, then perhaps there is a fairy nearby.

# Superstitions And Beliefs
## Animals/Birds

• It is said that if a woman or her cow are distracted during milking, the cow will give no milk which would be a serious loss to the family who owned it. To prevent this, a red tape is tied over the animal's head, a procedure known as 'blinking the cow'.

• A cow calves only once a year and is usually fed oaten meal for its health. When it has calved, it is the woman of the house who has the first milking of her and a tin can with an old sixpence coin inside it is used to bring good luck. The calf is usually kept in the family house for warmth for a while.

• If a frog enters your house it is considered to be an omen of death.

• Around the last ten days of April, farmers and the local folk usually await the arrival of the cuckoo:
*Cuckoo comes in April,*
*Sings her song in May,*
*Whistles her tune in the middle of June,*
*And then she flies away.*
Your fortune is determined by where you are standing on hearing the cuckoo's song. If you happen to be standing on firm ground it means you will live another year. If you happen to be standing on grass it means you are soon to be buried.

Also, when you hear the cuckoo, you are supposed to walk three miles in the direction you are going to maintain good luck. Only if you are heading towards the sea may you take a detour.

• If a raven happens to fly low past your window when you are counting money it is a sign of the Devil.

• If a house martin happens to take possession of a hair from your head, and uses it to make its nest, this means very good fortune will accompany you always.

# Cures And Treatments

• The cure for a bad throat and a cough was to get one stallion donkey and feed it oaten bread. Then feed the invalid whatever dropped from the donkey's mouth and pass him or her under the animal three times for a full cure.

• Giving an invalid a loaf of bread boiled with milk and Epsom salts, or making him or her lie in a bed of nettles, was said to be a cure for anything.

• When a cow has a 'slip-tail' or weak spine, the condition must be cured or the animal will die. The cure was to cut a hole in the tail of the cow and put a garlic seed inside. The tail was then covered with a cloth and left for a few days until the animal was healed.

• The cure for arthritis was to fetch a bunch of strong nettles and sting the affected area of the invalid. A couple of days later the person should be cured.

• The cure for mumps was for a married couple to lead the invalid across a stream wearing a donkey bridle! This would only work, however, when the wife's maiden name was the same as her married name.

• The slime from a snail was believed to be very good for curing warts.

• There is a sweat house situated at Lecamy, one kilometre from Noon's Bridge on the Moville to Carndonagh road, and within sight of the Culdaff-Carrowmore road. It is approximately seven feet in height and remains perfectly intact in a bee-hive shaped structure. Decades ago it was used as a sort of sauna bath for the cure of rheumatism and temporary madness. A turf fire was lit inside to warm the building. When the fire had burned out and the remnants cleaned, the sufferer was brought inside. The entrance to the sweat house was sealed off and the sufferer stayed in there to sweat it out until he or she was cured.

# Death

The subject of death frightened and mystified people and some very peculiar beliefs and customs sprang from this most ancient of fears.

• Well-known death signals included hearing a banshee wail, the banging of timber (apparently the fairies making someone's coffin), a series of knocks on one's door or window, or from seeing lights around a neighbour's house.

• It was traditional for the family of the bereaved to stop their clocks and turn all the mirrors to the walls at the time of death. Occasionally a window was opened.

• The corpse was kept for two days and two nights after the death at a 'wake' and visiting neighbours and family were provided with tea, food, tobacco and whiskey. Twelve ounces of tobacco were meant to be smoked to signify the twelve apostles.

• The most direct route to the church or graveyard was deliberately not taken to delay the final inevitable moment. As soon as the procession left the dead person's home, the woman of the house would immediately undo all the procedures required for the laying out of the corpse. If chairs had been borrowed to sit upon they would be put outside, but if the coffin had rested on them they would be placed upside down on the street in front of the house. A sip of whiskey was consumed by each member remaining in the house.

• The day after the funeral all blankets and sheets relating to the corpse were washed and cleaned.

• It was considered disrespectful to speak ill of the dead. People used to say: 'May God rest him' or 'May he rest in peace' and this is still prevalent today.

# Fairies

There are several categories of fairies which can be found alone or in groups and these include:

• The banshee. A silver-haired woman who releases a piercing wail predicting death. She is said to follow only families of true Irish descent and those with 'Mac' in their surnames. Normally, a fairy woman is a lot taller than a fairy man, yet the banshee is described as being quite small.

• The clarchain. A type of fairy recognisable by the silver buckles on his shoes. If you happen to spy him at night, chances are he is dancing and getting drunk.

- An fear dearg (the red man). This character is dressed all in red with a strong sense of mischief and no sense of humour.

- The leprechaun. The most notorious of the wee folk, the leprechaun is said to be a pipe-smoking shoemaker known to be good to housewives. He is also regarded as a miser who guards the legendary crock of gold with an air of mischief and liveliness.

- The pooka. Not much is known about this creature except that it is meant to take on the form of a bull, bird or goat.

- Trooping fairies. This group keep themselves to themselves. They are generally amicable and gentle creatures. One flaw in their character is that they have a fondness for stealing away children.

- A changeling. A creature with dark, wrinkled skin which is left in the place of a young child abducted by the fairies. A rational explanation can be traced to the disease of tuberculosis which attacked the body very rapidly leaving it looking aged and haggard. People were so shocked at the dramatic change in the child's appearance that they were convinced the fairies had substituted a changeling in its place.

- To protect a baby from the fairies when no one was in the house, either a fire was lit or iron tongs were placed across the top of the cradle preventing him or her from being stolen away by the wee folk.

- Fairies are supposed to congregate where three townlands meet and many sightings of fairies are near such sites, often with a 'fairy tree' or 'fairy bush' growing close by.

- It is believed that if anyone cut the whitethorn tree (known as the 'magic tree') or the blackthorn or hawthorn bush, their cattle and/or children would develop a fever, get sick and possibly die.

• It was advisable, on occasion, to placate the fairies by giving them some type of gift or present. For example, if poteen was being distilled it was customary to give the top of the brew to the fairies by leaving it in a crack in the rocks, otherwise the poteen would fail. It is a scientific fact that the skin or skimmings (the first of the poteen when it starts to bubble) must be removed as it is not only poisonous but the rest of the chemical process will not take place if this is not done. Those who removed the skin and drank it usually died, which some believed to be the fairies' retribution.

• If you were generous to the fairies on Hallowe'en night they would see to it that you would receive your reward during the rest of the year.

## Fishing And The Sea

• The sighting of mermaids is thought of as a premonition of death by mariners of all types.

• Friday is regarded as an unlucky day for sailors to go out to sea, possibly because Friday was the day of the Crucifixion.

• Holy water was always taken out to the boat as a blessing to safeguard the crew and their catch.

• A 'Jonah' is a person who can catch no fish no matter where he is, or what size of net or type of bait he uses, even though all around him are taking an average catch. A 'Super Jonah' is the kind whose ill fate affects all the fishermen in the vicinity and it does not take them long to banish this unfortunate being from the waters.

• Salmon and herring were known as 'gentle fish' (fairy fish), and if a woman went out fishing in the salmon season neither salmon nor herring would be caught.

• Butter was not allowed on bread nor bacon eaten on boats until about ten years ago.

• To mention certain types of animals, for example pigs, cows and rabbits, was bad luck while at sea, possibly because they were land animals which couldn't swim. Bacon and pigs were collectively called 'Curly Tails' instead.

- To whistle on board a boat spelt disaster; it meant that the person responsible was whistling up a storm.

## General

- The evening of 31 January each year is known as Saint Bridget's Eve and on that day the head of the family would cut rushes and spread them on the table like a tablecloth. A meal of mashed potatoes and butter was then served and eaten with each person in the house taking their turn at mashing the potatoes.

Crosses were made for every door of the house and the outhouses for the animals. They were then put in a basket and placed outside with some cloth awaiting the blessing of Saint Bridget. Next day the family went to Mass and when they had returned they would put the crosses at every entrance. The cloth was known as 'Brat Bhríde' and was kept for use in case of sickness while the crosses remained above the doors until the following year.

- Considerable care was always taken when people gave each other gifts. If the gift was a fish, salt was put on its tail. If a neighbour came for a live coal, he was required to put a turf on the fire before he left the house as people thought that they might be giving away their good fortune otherwise.

- All Souls' Day carried its own traditions. When raking out the fire it was customary to leave some ashes in the hearth and the following morning, if the fairies had visited, footprints would be visible. In every household, a jug or dish of water would be put on the kitchen table for the souls to drink on their journey to heaven.

- It is said that if a pregnant woman looks into the face of the devil her children will be cross-eyed.

## Hallowe'en

Some of the traditional games included foretelling the future which could be done in many different ways.

- If you were to eat an apple in front of a mirror you would see your future partner in the reflection.

45

• If you took a lantern down to a stream you would again see your future partner, this time in the water.

• If a young woman wanted to know if her lover(s) were faithful, she would put three nuts on the bars of the fire grate, naming the nuts after her lovers. If a nut cracked or jumped this proved that her lover was unfaithful. If a nut began to blaze it meant that her lover had a high regard for her. If a nut burned together with the one she had named for herself it meant that she and her lover were destined to marry.

• Another way for women to discover the identity of their future love was to bind twigs from a holly bush with silken thread to represent a couple. The twigs were placed on a circle of clay and a live coal was positioned inside the circle. If the twigs caught fire it signified that the couple would someday have a romantic relationship.

• If a snail was placed on a plate of flour, covered with another plate, and left until morning, its tracks would spell out the name of the future husband.

• It was also traditional to bake a cake for Hallowe'en containing coins and other items. Today we have the barmbrack variety which usually includes a ring for luck. In the past the ring signified marriage, a thimble meant you'd become a spinster, a button that you'd remain a bachelor and to receive a coin meant future wealth.

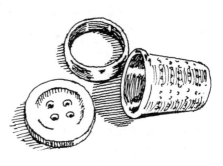

• In the evening a ceremonial supper was held during which salt and meal were mixed and rubbed into the crown of the head, in the name of the Father, the Son and the Holy Ghost. This was said to prevent the fairies stealing you away if you ventured outdoors.

## New Year

• Everything had to be cleaned, washed and left exceptionally tidy on New Year's Eve. It was believed that if you left your dirty dishes to the following day you would be lumbered with toil and labour for the coming year.

• To ensure good luck during the whole year, nothing was taken out of the dwelling house on New Year's Day. Ashes remained in the hearth and washing water remained in a large receptacle. Early in the morning, water was taken from the well and salt was added. Each person took three sips to invoke the protection of the Holy Trinity and the remainder was given to the livestock.

• The eldest of the family was responsible for going outside to bring in the turf on the morning of New Year's Day.

# Red-headed Women

• If a red-headed woman was 'ceilidhing' on New Year's Eve it was customary for her to bring along a piece of coal. When she entered the neighbour's premises she would have to give the piece of coal to the man of the house before she was allowed across the doorstep, but only if she was the first red head to visit.

• If a red-headed woman was sighted by a fisherman on his way to sea it was believed to be exceptionally bad luck, so the man would turn on his heels and go home as no fish would be caught that day.

• For a man to meet a red-headed woman on the way to his wedding was an omen of bad luck and the marriage was doomed from the start.

• There is a belief that if a red-headed princess who dwelt in a castle fell out with her lover and refused to speak to him for several months she would be turned into a beautiful black cat that would be coveted by all but her former friend.

# GUILDHALL PRESS

## Publications

Derry's Walls by Paul Hippsley

O'Doherty Historic Trail by Murray Dougherty

George Walker by George Sweeney

The Siege Of Derry – 1689 by Peter Mc Cartney

There Was Music There In The Derry Air
by Anne Mulkeen Murray

What About The Workers! by George Sweeney

Talk Of The Town & The Folly Up
by Seamus McConnell

Derry Jail by Colm M. Cavanagh

Across The Foyle by Anne Murray

The Best Of Jed – Compiled by Sinead Coyle

Derry's Shirt Tale by Geraldine McCarter

Springtown Chronicles by Seamus McConnell

Church, Chapel & Meeting House
by Art Byrne and Marilyn Frazer

Hiring Fairs & Farm Workers In North-West Ireland
by Michael O'Hanlon

Parade Of Phantoms (Revised edition) by Peter Mc Cartney

The War Years: Derry 1939-45
by Guildhall Press/Heritage Library

"Oh How We Danced" by Harry McCourt

Half-Hanged MacNaghten by Darinagh Boyle

Meeting The European Challenge
by Peter Mc Cartney and Sharon Porter